DRUG ADDICTION AND RECOVERY

Prescription Drugs

Prescription Drugs

H.W. Poole

SERIES CONSULTANT

SARA BECKER, Ph.D.

Brown University School of Public Health
Warren Alpert Medical School

MASON CREST

Mason Crest
450 Parkway Drive, Suite D
Broomall, PA 19008
www.masoncrest.com

MTM Publishing, Inc.
www.mtmpublishing.com

President: Valerie Tomaselli
Vice President, Book Development: Hilary Poole
Designer: Annemarie Redmond
Copyeditor: Peter Jaskowiak
Editorial Assistant: Andrea St. Aubin

Series ISBN: 978-1-4222-3598-0
Hardback ISBN: 978-1-4222-3610-9
E-Book ISBN: 978-1-4222-8254-0

Library of Congress Cataloging-in-Publication Data
Names: Poole, Hilary W., author.
Title: Prescription drugs / by H.W. Poole.
Description: Broomall, PA : Mason Crest, [2017] | Series: Drug addiction and
    recovery | Includes bibliographical references and index.
Identifiers: LCCN 2016004069| ISBN 9781422236109 (hardback) | ISBN
    9781422235980 (series) | ISBN 9781422282540 (ebook)
Subjects: LCSH: Medication abuse—Juvenile literature. | Drugs—Juvenile
    literature.
Classification: LCC HV5809.5 .P66 2017 | DDC 362.29/9—dc23
LC record available at http://lccn.loc.gov/2016004069

Printed and bound in the United States of America.

First printing
9 8 7 6 5 4 3 2 1

TABLE OF CONTENTS

Key Icons to Look for:

Words to Understand: These words with their easy-to-understand definitions will increase the reader's understanding of the text, while building vocabulary skills.

Sidebars: This boxed material within the main text allows readers to build knowledge, gain insights, explore possibilities, and broaden their perspectives by weaving together additional information to provide realistic and holistic perspectives.

Research Projects: Readers are pointed toward areas of further inquiry connected to each chapter. Suggestions are provided for projects that encourage deeper research and analysis.

Text-Dependent Questions: These questions send the reader back to the text for more careful attention to the evidence presented there.

Educational Videos: Readers can view videos by scanning our QR codes, providing them with additional educational content to supplement the text. Examples include news coverage, moments in history, speeches, iconic sports moments and much more!

Series Glossary of Key Terms: This back-of-the-book glossary contains terminology used throughout the series. Words found here increase the reader's ability to read and comprehend higher-level books and articles in this field.

SERIES INTRODUCTION

Many adolescents in the United States will experiment with alcohol or other drugs by time they finish high school. According to a 2014 study funded by the National Institute on Drug Abuse, about 27 percent of 8th graders have tried alcohol, 20 percent have tried drugs, and 13 percent have tried cigarettes. By 12th grade, these rates more than double: 66 percent of 12th graders have tried alcohol, 50 percent have tried drugs, and 35 percent have tried cigarettes.

Adolescents who use substances experience an increased risk of a wide range of negative consequences, including physical injury, family conflict, school truancy, legal problems, and sexually transmitted diseases. Higher rates of substance use are also associated with the leading causes of death in this age group: accidents, suicide, and violent crime. Relative to adults, adolescents who experiment with alcohol or other drugs progress more quickly to a full-blown substance use disorder and have more co-occurring mental health problems.

The National Survey on Drug Use and Health (NSDUH) estimated that in 2015 about 1.3 million adolescents between the ages of 12 and 17 (5 percent of adolescents in the United States) met the medical criteria for a substance use disorder. Unfortunately, the vast majority of these

IF YOU NEED HELP NOW . . .

SAMHSA's National Helpline provides referrals for mental-health or substance-use counseling.
1-800-662-HELP (4357) or https://findtreatment.samhsa.gov

SAMHSA's National Suicide Prevention Lifeline provides crisis counseling by phone or online, 24-hours-a-day and 7 days a week.
1-800-273-TALK (8255) or http://www.suicidepreventionlifeline.org

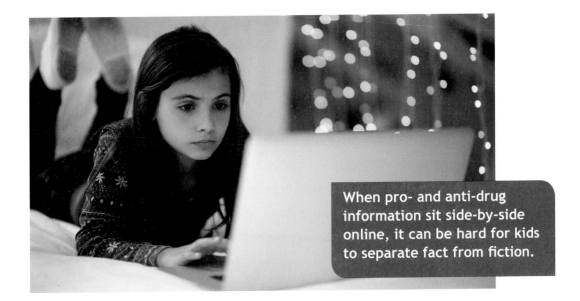

When pro- and anti-drug information sit side-by-side online, it can be hard for kids to separate fact from fiction.

adolescents did not receive treatment. Less than 10 percent of those with a diagnosis received specialty care, leaving 1.2 million adolescents with an unmet need for treatment.

The NSDUH asked the 1.2 million adolescents with untreated substance use disorders why they didn't receive specialty care. Over 95 percent said that they didn't think they needed it. The other 5 percent reported challenges finding quality treatment that was covered by their insurance. Very few treatment providers and agencies offer substance use treatment designed to meet the specific needs of adolescents. Meanwhile, numerous insurance plans have "opted out" of providing coverage for addiction treatment, while others have placed restrictions on what is covered.

Stigma about substance use is another serious problem. We don't call a person with an eating disorder a "food abuser," but we use terms like "drug abuser" to describe individuals with substance use disorders. Even treatment providers often unintentionally use judgmental words, such as describing urine screen results as either "clean" or "dirty." Underlying this language is the idea that a substance use disorder is some kind of moral failing or character flaw, and that people with these disorders deserve blame or punishment for their struggles.

And punish we do. A 2010 report by CASA Columbia found that in the United States, 65 percent of the 2.3 million people in prisons and jails met medical criteria for a substance use disorder, while another 20 percent had histories of substance use disorders, committed their crimes while under the influence of alcohol or drugs, or committed a substance-related crime. Many of these inmates spend decades in prison, but only 11 percent of them receive any treatment during their incarceration. Our society invests significantly more money in punishing individuals with substance use disorders than we do in treating them.

At a basic level, the ways our society approaches drugs and alcohol—declaring a "war on drugs," for example, or telling kids to "Just Say No!"—reflect a misunderstanding about the nature of addiction. The reality is that addiction is a disease that affects all types of people—parents and children, rich and poor, young and old. Substance use disorders stem from a complex interplay of genes, biology, and the environment, much like most physical and mental illnesses.

The way we talk about recovery, using phrases like "kick the habit" or "breaking free," also misses the mark. Substance use disorders are chronic, insidious, and debilitating illnesses. Fortunately, there are a number of effective treatments for substance use disorders. For many patients, however, the road is long and hard. Individuals recovering from substance use disorders can experience horrible withdrawal symptoms, and many will continue to struggle with cravings for alcohol or drugs. It can be a daily struggle to cope with these cravings and stay abstinent. A popular saying at Alcoholics Anonymous (AA) meetings is "one day at a time," because every day of recovery should be respected and celebrated.

There are a lot of incorrect stereotypes about individuals with substance use disorders, and there is a lot of false information about the substances, too. If you do an Internet search on the term "marijuana," for instance, two top hits are a web page by the National Institute on Drug Abuse and a page operated by Weedmaps, a medical and recreational marijuana dispensary. One of these pages publishes scientific information and one publishes pro-marijuana articles. Both pages have a high-quality, professional appearance. If you had never heard of either organization, it would be hard to know which to trust. It can be really difficult for the average person, much less the average teenager, to navigate these waters.

The topics covered in this series were specifically selected to be relevant to teenagers. About half of the volumes cover the types of drugs that they are most likely to hear about or to come in contact with. The other half cover important issues related to alcohol and other drug use (which we refer to as "drug use" in the titles for simplicity). These books cover topics such as the causes of drug use, the influence of drug use on the family, drug use and the legal system, drug use and mental health, and treatment options. Many teens will either have personal experience with these issues or will know someone who does.

This series was written to help young people get the facts about common drugs, substance use disorders, substance-related problems, and recovery. Accurate information can help adolescents to make better decisions. Students who are educated can help each other to better understand the risks and consequences of drug use. Facts also go a long way to reducing the stigma associated with substance use. We tend to fear or avoid things that we don't understand. Knowing the facts can make it easier to support each other. For students who know someone struggling with a substance use disorder, these books can also help them know what to expect. If they are worried about someone, or even about themselves, these books can help to provide some answers and a place to start.

—Sara J. Becker, Ph.D., Assistant Professor (Research), Center for Alcohol and Addictions Studies, Brown University School of Public Health, Assistant Professor (Research), Department of Psychiatry and Human Behavior, Brown University Medical School

WORDS TO UNDERSTAND

chronic: something that recurs for a long time and doesn't get better.

diversion: when something changes course; in this context, when a drug created for medical purposes ends up used in some other way.

euphoria: great, almost overwhelming, pleasure.

neurotransmitter: a chemical in the brain that carries signals.

patent: a government document that certifies ownership of a unique invention or process.

regulations: rules that limit what companies or individuals are allowed to do.

sedatives: chemicals that are calming or cause sleep.

stimulants: chemicals that increase energy and wakefulness.

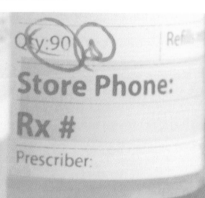

CHAPTER ONE

WHAT ARE PRESCRIPTION DRUGS?

Prescription medications are part of the fabric of American life. Uncountable numbers of lives have been improved because of these medicines. They fight cancer and AIDS. They help stave off heart attacks and strokes. And for about 70 million Americans who cope with chronic pain, prescription drugs can be the only thing that makes normal life possible. About 1 in 10 Americans takes some form of antidepressant on a regular basis, and countless suicides and other catastrophes have been averted thanks to these medications. There's no doubt, therefore, that prescription drugs save lives.

But too often, these same drugs are taken for purposes outside their intended use. Experts call this use **diversion**. And when diversion occurs, miracle drugs can turn into nightmares. According to the National Center for Health Statistics, more than 22,000 Americans died from prescription drug overdoses in 2013. That works out to 60 deaths every single day. And the problem is getting worse—that 2013 figure was nearly double what it was a decade earlier (see table on page 13). And these numbers don't include the many people struggling with addiction or the family members and friends who are also affected.

Troublingly, many of these users are young people. A national survey found that in 2013, almost 14 percent of 12th graders admitted to having used a prescription drug for "nonmedical" reasons.

This volume will discuss the three most frequently misused types of prescription drugs: painkillers such as Vicodin and OxyContin, sedatives such

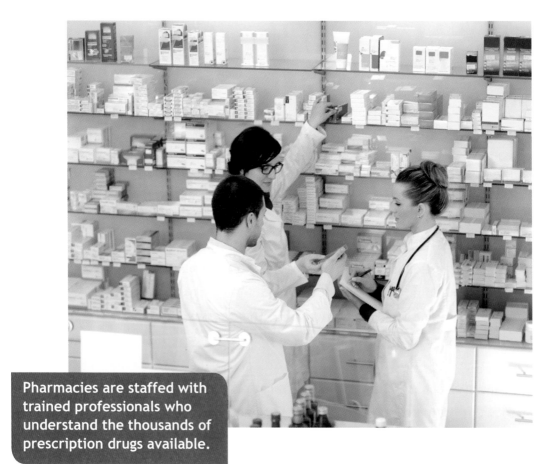

Pharmacies are staffed with trained professionals who understand the thousands of prescription drugs available.

OVERDOSE DEATHS FROM PRESCRIPTION VERSUS ILLEGAL DRUGS

	2003	2005	2007	2009	2011	2013
Prescription Drugs	12,640	15,352	19,601	20,848	22,810	22,767
Female	5,191	6,351	8,251	8,740	9,771	10,019
Male	7,449	9,001	11,350	12,108	13,039	12,748
Illegal Drugs	7,653	8,923	9,418	8,446	10,284	14,775
Female	1,854	2,251	2,301	2,043	2,636	3,707
Male	5,799	6,672	7,117	6,403	7,648	11,068

Source: National Center on Health Statistics. "Overdose Death Rates."
http://www.drugabuse.gov/related-topics/trends-statistics/overdose-death-rates.

as Valium and Quaaludes, and stimulants such as Adderall and Ritalin. But first, let's look back at the history of prescription drugs and discuss how they work.

THE EVOLUTION OF PRESCRIPTION DRUGS

At the dawn of the American Revolution, there were only about 400 doctors for the 2.4 million colonists. Many people didn't trust those doctors, and for good reason. Even Dr. Benjamin Rush, arguably colonial America's most respected doctor (and a signer of the Declaration of Independence), believed that most illnesses could be cured by removing large quantities of blood from his patients. Medical historians believe Rush accidentally killed many people, including none other than George Washington, with this bleeding technique.

America's understandable distrust of doctors set the stage, in the late 18th and 19th centuries, for the expansion of the patent medicine industry. In theory, a *patent medicine* should have unique healing ingredients— certainly, that's what the term *patent* implies. But despite their name, patent medicines were rarely unique and almost never patented. These homemade remedies usually contained large amounts of alcohol, cocaine, or some other mood-altering substance. For example, Dr. Fahrney's Teething Syrup for babies contained morphine, an addictive painkiller. The active ingredient in Dr. Bull's Cough Syrup was heroin. A cold remedy called Lungardia contained alcohol, turpentine, and kerosene.

These patent medicines were packaged with colorful labels and wild claims about all the many ills they could cure. The entrepreneurs who sold them, often by traveling from town to town, came to be called "snake-oil salesmen." And even though their products rarely worked, many of these hucksters made profits because of the addictive properties of their products. Users of Dr. Bull's Cough Syrup, in other words, may not have had very bad coughs at all.

From our 21st century perspective, it seems shocking that parents once soothed their babies with a tiny dose of morphine. How is it possible that these clearly dangerous patent medicines were available to anyone who could pay for them? Simply put, the strict **regulations** that now govern our access to drugs did not exist at the time.

Regulation of the pharmaceutical industry began with the Pure Food and Drug Act of 1906. That law's focus had less to do with prescriptions and more to do with labeling and transparency about ingredients. The act was replaced by the more far-reaching Federal Food, Drug, and Cosmetic Act (FFDCA) of 1938. But it was the Durham-Humphrey Amendment of 1951 that clearly established a legal category of drugs that could only be sold with a doctor's prescription. The act defined a prescription drug as any medication that "because of its toxicity or other potentiality for harmful effect . . . is not safe for use except under the supervision of a practitioner licensed by law to administer such drug."

The amendment was not without controversy. Pharmaceutical companies objected to the government's attempt to limit the number of people who could buy their products. Others complained that the

In 1915, a crowd looks at a pharmacy display, where a pianist is endorsing a stomach medicine called Digestit. The man has been reportedly been playing piano for over 60 hours straight to show how well Digestit works.

prescription-only category was unfair because it forced patients to not just pay for the drugs, but also for the doctor's visits needed to acquire the prescriptions in the first place.

The goal of Durham-Humphrey—not to mention the many additional regulations that followed—was to protect the public by limiting access to potentially dangerous medications. Unfortunately, America's current epidemic of prescription drug misuse suggests that these regulations have not been completely successful.

Still, regulations on prescriptions are an important way to at least *attempt* to keep powerful medicines where they belong. A doctor or other specially trained health-care provider must write out the prescription on a form, which is usually called in or taken to a pharmacist—also specially trained—who can

I'D LIKE TO BUY THE WORLD MEDICAL WINE

A "medical wine" introduced in Europe in 1869 was called Vin Mariani. It was essentially a blend of alcohol and stimulants. Copycat "medical" beverages soon became popular in the United States as well. One of the most popular was invented by a pharmacist named John Pemberton. Makers of Pemberton's sweet, cocaine-based beverage eventually dropped the medical claims, and their product became famous all over the world as Coca-Cola. The soda no longer contains cocaine, of course, but it does have caffeine, which is a legal stimulant.

An advertisement for Coca Cola from the 1890s.

dole out the drug in the correct amount. In theory (although, as we know, not always in practice), this system should make it possible for people who need drugs to get them, while preventing misuse by others.

Prescription drugs are just one part of the overall picture. A medicine that can be bought without a prescription is called an over-the-counter (OTC) medication. Total U.S. sales for OTC drugs are more than $40 billion dollars annually. Although they are, by definition, less dangerous than prescription drugs, OTC drugs do still have the potential for misuse. For more on this topic, please see another volume in this set, *Over-the-Counter Drugs*.

HOW DO MEDICINES WORK?

Medicine gets into the body through the blood stream. This can be accomplished by swallowing a tablet or liquid, by injecting the drug directly into the veins, by inhaling the drug, or by wearing a patch that pushes the drug into the skin. Regardless of the method, the goal is the same—to get the medication circulating in the blood. Swallowing a drug is the slowest way to get it into the bloodstream, while injecting it is the quickest. This is why users of prescription painkillers sometimes progress from swallowing painkillers to crushing the pills up and injecting or snorting them.

Different medicines work in different ways, but for the purposes of this discussion, we will focus on drugs that affect the brain. The human brain is essentially a communications center, and drugs work by changing the way this communication center functions. In the brain, messages are passed back and forth via chemicals called **neurotransmitters**. Having more or less of a particular neurotransmitter will result in changes in how the brain passes information from one part to another. This, in turn, will affect how a person feels and behaves.

There are a few different ways that drugs affect neurotransmitters. Some drugs, such as marijuana, contain chemicals that actually mimic

USE AND MISUSE?

When we picture a "drug user," we often imagine someone whose life is a mess—like the "junkies" or "meth heads" portrayed on television. But that's not an accurate picture of what people who use drugs actually look like.

Prescription drugs can be misused in a few different ways. When people take a prescription medicine without actually having a prescription—maybe they get it from friends, sneak it from parents, or buy it online—that's clearly misuse. It's also possible for someone to misuse his or her own prescription. Activities such as taking more of a drug than what is prescribed, taking it more frequently than instructed, or taking a medicine in combination with some other drug can all qualify as misuse. People who misuse prescription drugs don't necessarily look like characters on TV. They're just people—maybe even people you know.

the behavior of natural neurotransmitters, so the user's brain receives a flood of these extra chemicals. Other drugs, such as cocaine, prevent neurotransmitters from being absorbed by the brain, leading to an increase in the overall amount.

Commonly misused prescription drugs have the potential for long-term and even permanent effects. The chapters that follow will discuss the specific impacts of painkillers, tranquilizers, and stimulants.

DOPAMINE

If you try something new—a new food, a new activity, whatever it might be—and you enjoy it, chances are you'll want to repeat that new thing in the future. On a chemical level, the reason you want to repeat the experience is because you enjoyed a spike in your dopamine levels.

Dopamine is a neurotransmitter, which is a type of chemical that passes information from one part of the brain to another. The brain registers all pleasure the same way, whether it originates with eating a burger, scoring a goal, or taking a drug. The experience of pleasure is a result of the dopamine. The more you enjoy something, the more dopamine you are likely to have in your system.

Since dopamine is part of normal human function, you might wonder why using drugs to raise dopamine levels is even a problem. Don't drugs just re-create a natural process? The answer is yes and no. It's true that everyone—the drug user and non-user alike—experiences daily changes in dopamine levels. However, drugs tend to raise the levels far above what ordinary experiences would do. That's a big part of what makes drugs tempting. But when used repeatedly, the brain adjusts to these inflated levels, producing less dopamine on its own or making it harder for the brain to absorb

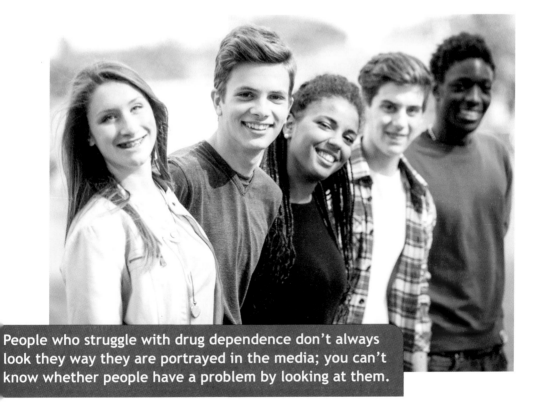

People who struggle with drug dependence don't always look they way they are portrayed in the media; you can't know whether people have a problem by looking at them.

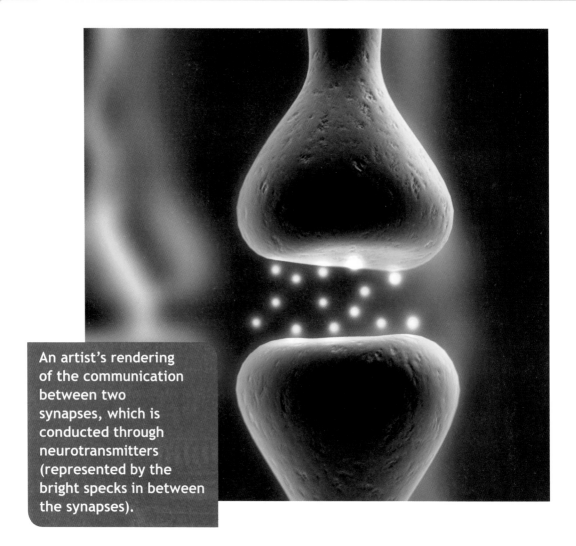

An artist's rendering of the communication between two synapses, which is conducted through neurotransmitters (represented by the bright specks in between the synapses).

dopamine. These adaptations are similar to turning the volume down on a radio. In addition, a user can get used to surges in dopamine and come to expect the euphoria of drugs. This can make it extremely difficult for regular users to cope with "normal" (that is, not artificially inflated) rewards.

"GOOD" DRUGS AND "BAD" DRUGS

One of the biggest dangers of prescription medications is the assumption that they aren't dangerous because they are made and sold by legitimate companies. People tell themselves that prescription drugs are completely different from the ones sold on a street corner.

There is one tiny element of truth here. Prescription drugs are safer than illegal drugs in the sense that they are more pure. As long as they were made by a reputable company, then they were not "cut" with potentially toxic additives, as "street" or "hard" drugs often are. Also, there is usually (but not always) far less physical danger involved in acquiring prescription drugs.

But in every other sense, there is no real difference between hard drugs and the ones that come from the pharmacy. The popular painkiller called OxyContin has the same chemistry as heroin. Medications for attention-deficit hyperactivity disorder (ADHD) are members of the same drug family as both cocaine and methamphetamine (meth). And *all* the drugs covered in this volume can be highly dangerous if they are used in ways other than how they are prescribed. A perfect example is prescription sleep aids with

At times it can be difficult for doctors to tell whether patients who ask for pain medications truly need them or not.

DOCTOR SHOPPING

By definition, the drugs discussed in this volume should only be taken under a doctor's orders. The reasoning behind this is clear: in the interest of public safety, laws try to ensure that dangerous drugs are only used when they are absolutely needed. But this assumes that a doctor can know precisely what a patient does and does not need. In the real world, it doesn't always work this way.

There is no test that can *prove* whether or not a patient is in pain. There's also no way for a doctor to know how many other doctors a patient has visited. So it is something of a guessing game as to whether or not patients are being honest about their need for medication. People seeking prescription drugs for nonmedical uses have been known to lie to doctors about their symptoms. They have also been known to visit more than one doctor, trying to obtain prescriptions from each one. This practice is called "doctor shopping."

Different states have different laws regarding doctor shopping, but it most places, it is considered a criminal act to lie to a health-care provider in order to obtain prescription medicine. Another problem with doctor shopping is that the practice can make health-care providers deeply suspicious of *anyone* who comes in looking for pain medicine. Sometimes people with legitimate medical needs have trouble getting treated, because doctors have had so many run-ins with doctor-shoppers. Many states are now cracking down on doctor shopping by creating prescription medicine registries and enacting harsh penalties for individuals caught in the act.

brand names like Ambien and Lunesta: used properly, they are generally safe and nonaddictive. But used improperly—in too-large amounts or mixed with other drugs—they can be risky and even deadly.

If prescription drugs are misused, it doesn't matter whether they were purchased in a dark alley or a well-lit pharmacy. These medications contain powerful chemicals that can save lives or destroy them.

TEXT-DEPENDENT QUESTIONS

1. What's the difference between OTC drugs and prescription drugs?
2. How does a drug like cocaine affect the brain, and how is it different from the way a drug like marijuana affects the brain?
3. How are prescription drugs like or unlike illegal drugs?

RESEARCH PROJECT

Download a copy of *Monitoring the Future,* a wide-ranging study that collects surveys of American teenagers on the subject of drug use (it is available at http://www.monitoringthefuture.org/pubs/monographs/mtf-vol1_2014.pdf). Look at chapter 10, which is the one covering prescription drugs in general, and ADHD medication in particular. Study the ADHD medication tables and make some observations about trends in stimulant use over time. Consider questions like these:

- When and where have the greatest increases in misuse taken place?
- What ages and ethnic groups have experienced the greatest rise in misuse of stimulants?
- Where do most teenagers get the stimulants to misuse?
- How do most teenagers perceive what their friends are doing?
- What do these trends suggest to you about the future?

WORDS TO UNDERSTAND

antagonist: a substance that interferes with or reverses a biological response.

central nervous system: the brain and spine; the system that controls breathing and other vital functions.

clinical: in a medical setting.

dependent: having a great need for something.

gastrointestinal: having to do with the stomach and digestion.

general anesthetic: a drug that shuts down the entire body, used for surgery.

receptor: a spot on the surface of a cell that "catches" specific chemicals.

recreationally: doing something just for fun.

synthetic: human-made.

tolerance: needing more of a drug to get the same effect.

withdrawal: the physical reaction to the absence of a particular chemical or substance.

CHAPTER TWO

PAINKILLERS

For as long as there have been humans, there have been humans in pain. For just as long, we as a species have searched for ways to reduce that pain. Pain management continues to be a key part of modern medicine, and there is a huge number of different drugs available for this purpose. The following is a very brief overview of the major types.

OTC Pain Medication. Two of the most common types of pain medication are aspirin and ibuprofen. These are called NSAIDs, which stands for nonsteroidal anti-inflammatory drugs. More than 30 million people use NSAIDs every day. Other popular over-the-counter (OTC) pain drugs include acetaminophen (called paracetamol in some countries) and naproxen. These drugs have minimal side effects and a low risk of addiction. But that's not to say they are entirely risk-free. Most notably, ibuprofen can damage the **gastrointestinal** system. NSAIDs can make you sick if you take too much, take them too often, or combine them with certain other drugs. Acetaminophen and alcohol is a particularly dangerous combination for the human liver. (For more on this topic, please refer to another volume in this set, *Over-the-Counter Drugs.*)

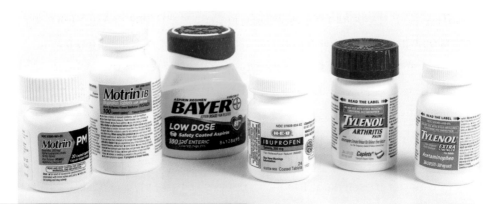

People looking for pain relief at the drug store have a lot of options available.

Prescription NSAIDS. Moving up the scale in terms of strength are NSAIDs that are only available by prescription. Brand names include Celebrex and Anaprox. These drugs all work more or less the same way as their OTC cousins, but they are stronger. They also have similar risks to the OTC versions—namely stomach, liver, and kidney problems. There is no euphoria with NSAIDs, so addiction is fairly unlikely. However, if people takes a strong prescription NSAID for a long period of time, they may start to believe they need it, and they will have a hard time stopping its use.

Opiates and Opioids. Opiates are painkillers that are derived from naturally occurring opium, while opioids are medications derived from synthetic or manufactured opium. They are extremely effective against short-term pain, but they tend to be highly addictive. Narcotics are the single-most misused category of prescription drug, and they are the focus of the rest of this chapter.

A SHORT HISTORY OF OPIATES AND OPIOIDS

Although the names and formulas have changed, the main source of pain control for humans has remained the same for over 5,000 years: *Papaver somniferum*, or the opium poppy. People in the ancient kingdom of Sumer, in what is now Iraq, called the poppy *Hul Gil*, "the flower of joy." It has been used both medicinally and **recreationally** ever since. Even in the 21st century, our most potent prescription painkillers are based on that same opium plant the Sumerians knew. That is why we still call these painkillers *opiates*.

Opium has always been effective in reducing pain; one preparation, called *laudanum*, first became popular in the Middle Ages. But it was the discovery of morphine in the early 1800s that truly made *Papaver somniferum* useful to medicine. Morphine, which was named after Morpheus, the Greek god of dreams, is extracted from the seed pod of the opium plant. It was first manufactured and sold on a wide scale in 1827 by a company called Merck (which remains a major player in the pharmaceutical industry).

The U.S. Civil War (1861–1865) resulted in about 1.5 million casualties in just four years, with 620,000 killed, 476,000 wounded, and another

A field of opium poppies.

400,000 captured or missing. Morphine was the primary—and arguably the only truly effective—weapon in the Civil War doctor's arsenal to treat wounded soldiers. Unfortunately, large numbers of Civil War veterans came home physically dependent on morphine.

Because of its effectiveness, morphine continues to be used in hospital settings as a legal prescription medication to this day. It is also an illegal street drug with many forms, including tablets and syrups, and many nicknames, such as "Miss Emma." Morphine is also the basis for other opiate medications, including oxycodone and methadone.

Like morphine, the drug called codeine comes directly from the opium plant. It was discovered by a French chemist in 1832 and has gone on to

Wounded soldiers who survived the Battle of Vicksburg, in the spring of 1863. (The woman in the doorway is a volunteer nurse.)

These heroin rocks were seized in a drug raid in Lashkar Gah, Afghanistan, in 2010.

become the most-used opiate in the world. It is a frequent ingredient in prescription cough medicines and in a combination drug called co-codamol, better known as Tylenol 3.

Heroin is a modified form of morphine that was invented by a chemist at the Bayer Company in 1895. Unlike the other opiate derivatives, heroin is never used as a prescription medication. (For more on heroin, please see another volume in this set, *Opioids: Heroin, OxyContin, and Painkillers*.)

The 20th century saw a further expansion in the number of opium-based drugs available. These are synthetic opiates, otherwise known as *opioids*. They work just like natural opiates and are chemically similar, but they are made in laboratories rather than directly from the opium plant. During the 20th century:

- Oxycodone was first used clinically in 1917.
- Hydrocodone (contemporary brand names include Vicodin, Lortab, Zamicet, Norco, and many more) and hydromorphone (Dilaudid, Exalgo, and more) were first made available in the 1920s.

- Fentanyl, an opiate that is about 15 times stronger than heroin, was originally created in 1960 as a **general anesthetic**.
- A blend of oxycodone and acetaminophen (brand names Percocet, Endocet, Xolox, and more) was approved for use in the 1970s.
- Buprenorphine was invented in the 1970s by researchers looking for a drug that would have the positive aspects of morphine without the negative effects (see below); it was not approved for use in the United States until 2002.
- OxyContin, which is an extended-release version of oxycodone, was first released in 1995 and then reformulated and re-released in 2013.

All these drugs first came to market as prescription pain medicine but many have ended up being diverted for nonmedical use. Today, prescription painkillers are among the most misused of all drugs: 10 times as many people misuse prescription painkillers than use heroin. Prescription painkillers are also among the deadliest drugs. Chapter one mentioned that about 60 people die from prescription drug overdoses every day; about two-thirds of those deaths involve painkillers.

FIGHTING OPIATES WITH OPIATES

Opiates and opioids have long presented a dilemma for health-care providers. On the one hand, the drugs are extremely effective; in fact, few if any other pain medications can even come close. On the other hand, opiates are also extremely addictive. Many scientists have worked hard to find alternatives that are as good as morphine at pain management but are not as risky for people's long-term well-being.

In the 1930s a group of German scientists created an opiate called methadone. Methadone eases pain, but it does not provide the euphoric feelings that make people crave it. In theory, this should make methadone less likely to be misused. In the 1960s, methadone began to be used as replacement therapy for people with heroin addiction. Instead of taking heroin, patients would receive scheduled doses of methadone. This would stave off the very unpleasant withdrawal symptoms but would not get them "high" the way heroin would. (Methadone is also prescribed for reasons other than heroin withdrawal, but drug treatment is its most famous use.)

Even though methadone doesn't get people high, it remains quite addictive in the physical sense. People who take methadone for long periods of time can develop a tolerance to it, which means they need to keep increasing their dose of the drug. Some patients end up essentially trading an addiction to heroin for an addiction to methadone. Another concern is that methadone stays in the body for quite a long time.

SIGNS OF PAINKILLER OVERDOSE

Whether it's a heroin addict in an alley or a lonesome celebrity in a hotel, stereotypes of painkiller overdoses usually involve some kind of dramatic—and often shady—situation. The reality is much different. A real overdose can be as simple as a grandmother who forgot she'd already taken her pain medication. It can be a toddler who gets into the medicine cabinet and thinks the pills look like candy. It can be a teenager who decides to try "oxy" at a party, not realizing that the drug combined with the three beers she already drank could put her in a coma.

Regardless of the situation, there are symptoms of possible painkiller overdose that everyone should know:

- severe stomach pain, vomiting, or diarrhea
- intense drowsiness, dizziness, or confusion
- vital signs, such as breathing, pulse, and body temperature, that are either way too low or way too high

If these symptoms are present, get help immediately.

That can be a good thing, but it can also leave people vulnerable to overdoses. There are about 5,000 deaths from methadone overdose every year.

In the late 1970s, a similar drug, buprenorphine, came into use for treating opiate withdrawl. Buprenorphine is believed to be safer than methadone, but it also tends to be more expensive. A 2014 study in the journal *Addiction* suggested that it may be less effective: of the more than 1,200 adults in a drug treatment program, 74 percent of the methadone users successfully completed their program, as opposed to only 46 percent of buprenorphine users.

Buprenorphine has also been combined with a drug called naloxone (brand name Narcan). Naloxone is an opiate antagonist, meaning that it

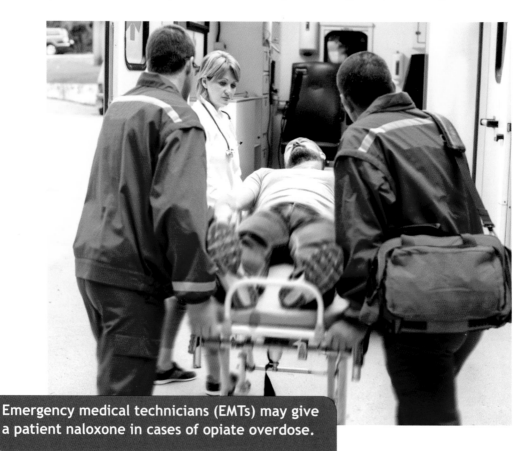

Emergency medical technicians (EMTs) may give a patient naloxone in cases of opiate overdose.

DEATHS FROM PAINKILLERS: Prescription Opioids versus Illegal Drugs, 2011 (Deaths per 100,000 People)

Age group	Deaths from opioid painkillers	Deaths from illegal drugs
15 to 24	3.7	2.2
25 to 34	7.1	4.4
35 to 44	8.3	5.3
45 to 54	10.4	6.0
55 to 64	5.0	2.5
65 and older	1.0	0.3

Source: National Institute on Drug Abuse, "DrugFacts: Prescription and Over-the-Counter Medications," December 2014. http://www.drugabuse.gov/publications/drugfacts/prescription-over-counter-medications.

works against opiates, essentially reversing their effects. It works very quickly; in fact, naloxone is the medicine of choice in case of an overdose. When combined with buprenorphine, the blend is called suboxone, which is prescribed for long-term treatment (as opposed to the immediate emergency of an overdose). Unfortunately, even suboxone is at risk of diversion for nonmedical use.

EFFECTS OF PAIN MEDICATION

Pain can be *localized*, meaning that it is limited to one area of the body, like when you hit your thumb with a hammer. Or it can be *systemic*, meaning that the pain is throughout the body; if you've ever had the flu, that "achy all over" feeling was systemic. A few types of painkillers have localized effects—there are NSAID creams and gels, for example, that can be rubbed onto the skin to ease joint or muscle pain. But the opioid-based drugs discussed in this chapter are all systemic.

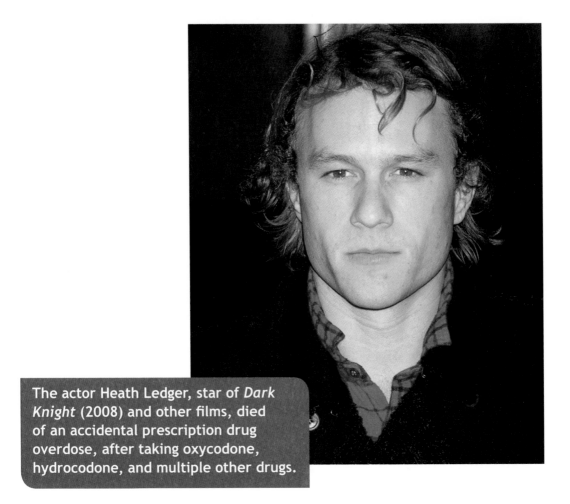

The actor Heath Ledger, star of *Dark Knight* (2008) and other films, died of an accidental prescription drug overdose, after taking oxycodone, hydrocodone, and multiple other drugs.

Humans have particular cells that were named "opioid **receptors**" specifically because of how they respond to the chemicals in these drugs. Opioid receptors exist throughout the **central nervous system** (CNS; comprising the brain and spinal cord) and also in the gastrointestinal system. Taking any of the narcotics mentioned in this chapter will affect every part of the body that has opioid receptors.

The chemicals in opiates and opioids cause a flood of dopamine, which is why users feel a euphoric "rush." The intensity varies depending on how the drug is ingested. Injection is the fastest way to get the chemicals into the bloodstream, resulting in the strongest "high" for the user. Unfortunately, this also makes injection the riskiest way to use these drugs, for the speed at which the drug spreads in the body makes an overdose more likely.

These drugs also affect the digestive system, where they can cause nausea and vomiting. Regular use will also cause constipation. In fact, one notoriously unpleasant result of opiate withdrawal is the tremendous diarrhea that occurs when opiates are no longer interfering with the intestines.

But it's the impact of opiates and opioids on the central nervous system that is arguably their most frightening trait. The CNS controls essential functions such as breathing. Opiates and opioids cause a slow-down (in medical terms, a *depression*) of breathing. This happens very quickly, and if too large a dose has been taken, it can cause a coma or death within a very short time. Depressed breathing means that less oxygen is reaching the brain; this is called *hypoxia*, which can lead to temporary or permanent brain damage. Unlike some of the other side effects, depression of breathing is not something that takes time to build up. It can happen the very first time someone uses a narcotic.

TEXT-DEPENDENT QUESTIONS

1. What are some different opiates? What do they have in common?
2. How can opiates be used to help treat opiate addiction?
3. What effects do opiates and opioids have on the body?

RESEARCH PROJECT

Find out more about the history of the prescription opiate industry in the United States. Create a timeline that features key moments, such the invention of various types of painkillers, as well as legislation introduced to control use.

WORDS TO UNDERSTAND

amnesia: loss of memory.

epilepsy: a brain disorder that causes convulsions.

hypnotics: drugs that cause sleep.

inhibitory: something that holds something else back or limits it.

pharmacological: having to do with drugs.

placebo: a medication that has no physical effect and is used to test whether new drugs actually work.

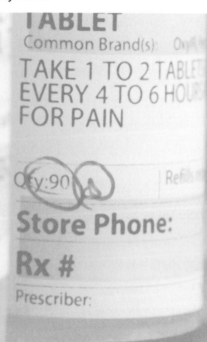

CHAPTER THREE

SEDATIVES AND HYPNOTICS

Painkillers are prescribed by doctors to help with problems in the body. A different category of drug, called sedatives, is used for certain problems of the mind—most notably, anxiety and panic. A closely related category is hypnotics, a term that refers not to a magician's trick but rather to substances that cause sleep. There is a lot of similarity between sedatives and hypnotics, both in terms of how the drugs work and how they are prescribed. That's why they are so frequently discussed together. You may also hear these drugs described as central nervous system (CNS) depressants, because that is mainly how they work—they slow down or impede parts of the CNS. There are several types:

- **Barbiturates.** The oldest class of sedative, barbiturates include phenobarbital, mephobarbital (brand name, Mebaral), and pentobarbital (Nembutal). Three other drugs—methaqualone (Quaaludes), meprobamate (Miltown), and carisoprodol (Soma)—are not barbiturates, but are considered "barbiturate-like," since they have essentially the same effects.

- **Benzodiazepines.** These are probably the most commonly misused group, and include diazepam (Valium), Librium, alprazolam (Xanax), and Rohypnol. They are considered safer and less addictive than barbiturates, but they can still present problems if taken for long periods or mixed with alcohol.

More than 30 percent of American adults report having trouble sleeping sometimes.

- **Nonbenzodiazepines.** These are sleep medications, including zolpidem (brand name, Ambien) and eszopiclone (Lunesta). Drug companies advertise these medications as "nonaddictive" because the body does not tend to become dependent on them. But it is possible to become *emotionally* dependent—to truly believe that you need them and have trouble going without them—even if there is no physical dependence.
- **Muscle relaxants.** This category of sedatives is not misused very often, with one major exception: dextromethorphan (DXM) is a sedative found in cough medicines. For many years it was available to anyone without a prescription, but in recent years age minimums have been enforced on its purchase. (For more on OTC pain medication, refer to then volume *Over-the-Counter Drugs* in this set.)

A BRIEF HISTORY OF SEDATIVES

All cultures have practices that encourage relaxation and better sleep. Native American medicine might recommend an herbal remedy, while traditional Chinese medicine might suggest acupuncture. Some people swear by yoga or a good book.

The pharmacological approach to anxiety and insomnia dates back to 1869, when a German professor named Matthias E. O. Liebreich realized that a substance called chloral hydrate could bring on relaxation and sleep. The barbiturate era began in 1903, when a pair of chemists published a paper on the chemical compound barbital. Soon the Bayer Company began selling barbital in the form of a sleep-aid called Veronal. Doctors found the drug was also helpful for psychiatric patients, and for people with epilepsy.

Meanwhile, scientists tinkered with the chemistry of barbiturates, finding that they could adjust the intensity and duration of their effects. More than 2,500 different blends were created, although most of them never went to market. The formulation called phenobarbital went on sale

Traditional Chinese medicine uses herbs and acupuncture to address problems like anxiety and insomnia.

in 1912 under the brand name Luminal. Its popularity led to phenobarbital being nicknamed the "king of the barbiturates." From this point until the 1950s, barbiturates were the treatment of choice for a wide range of problems, including anxiety, insomnia, and epilepsy. But they also have wide-acting effects on the CNS; in other words, while they do settle the parts of the brain that make people anxious, they also depress the part of the brains that control vital functions like breathing.

Doctors were not unaware of how addictive these drugs could be. In fact, within one year of Veronal being commercially available, the medical literature was already referring to "the Veronal habit." The highly addictive nature of these drugs—not to mention how easy it was to overdose on them—led U.S. lawmakers to begin regulating barbiturates in the late 1920s. The regulations did very little to dent the drugs' popularity, however, as there was a 400 percent *increase* in production after the laws went into effect. It was not just an American problem, either. There was, for example, a parallel rise in in barbiturate deaths (both accidental and intentional) in the United

Kingdom in the same period. It was clear that while barbiturates were (and continue to be) medically useful, they were also dangerous.

With the invention of benzodiazepines in the middle of the 20th century, doctors hoped a solution had been found: the first two were chlordiazepoxide (1955) and diazepam (1963), better known as Librium and Valium, respectively. Benzodiazepines do the same job as barbiturates, but they don't interfere with breathing the way their predecessors do. This makes them quite safe, as long as they are not combined with any other drug (especially alcohol). By 1977, benzodiazepines had become the most prescribed category of drug in the world (they have long since dropped down on that list, however). Initially, these drugs were believed to be nonaddictive, but experience suggests this was too optimistic a view. For example, clonazepam (Klonopin) was introduced in the mid 1970s as an epilepsy medication, but when it became popular recreationally, some people found themselves "doctor shopping" (see sidebar on page 22) to get more of the drug and stave off withdrawal.

The next evolution in sedative/hypnotic drugs was the invention of nonbenzodiazepines. As scientists learned more and more about how the CNS works, they were able to formulate increasingly more targeted drugs. Just as benzodiazepines had a narrower range of impact on the CNS than barbiturates, so did nonbenzodiazepines have a narrower range of effect than

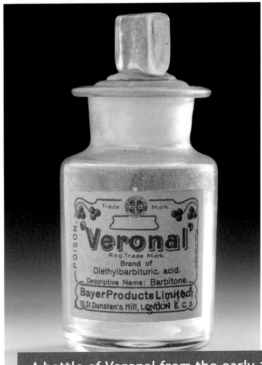

A bottle of Veronal from the early 1900s.

their predecessor. Some, such as zolpidem (Ambien; approved in 1993), are useful as sleep aids but not anti-anxiety medication, while alprazolam (Xanax; approved 1981) is the reverse.

ABUSING DRUGS, ABUSING OTHERS

When discussing the effects of drug use, the first things we think of are the ways drugs effect the person who takes them—including increased heart rate, feelings of euphoria, liver damage, and any number of possible negative and positive outcomes. The second way to think about drug use is how those drugs affect others, especially when those effects are negative. Drunk driving is an obvious instance of drug use hurting other people. But when it comes to sedatives, there's actually another, very disturbing way in which drug use impacts others—when sedatives are given to other people without their knowledge.

In the late 19th century, drugs called "knockout drops" were made from chloral hydrate, the first sedative. Today, sedatives such as Rohypnol, GHB, and ketamine are all sometimes used as "date rape drugs." The perpetrator sneaks a dose of the drug into a drink, which the victim consumes without knowing what's in it. In 1999 a Detroit teenager named Samantha Reid died—and her female friend was put on life-support—after being dosed with GHB. The young men who poisoned the women were found guilty of involuntary manslaughter and sentenced to from 5 to 15 years in prison.

The media is sometimes guilty of overstating threats, and it's difficult to get good statistics as to how often this kind of thing really occurs. But it does happen, and experts advise people, *especially* young women, to always get their own drinks at parties and keep a close eye on them, just to be safe.

EFFECTS OF SEDATIVES AND HYPNOTICS

Most sedatives and hypnotics work by affecting a neurotransmitter called GABA, which is an amino acid that is vital to CNS function. GABA is what's called an **inhibitory** neurotransmitter, meaning it slows things down. Drugs in the sedative/hypnotic class make GABA more effective in doing its job. This is why the drugs work so well for anxiety and insomnia—they force overactive brains to slow down. They are also good for surgery, again because they keep patients from being aware of what's happening. But too much GABA can shut down the CNS completely, causing coma or death.

Altering the CNS will have a wide range of effects on the rest of the body. These vary in intensity, depending on the type of sedative and how much was taken. Common physical effects are:

- drowsiness
- impaired motor skills (for example, eye-hand coordination and balance)
- slurred speech
- stupor (extremely dulled senses)
- amnesia
- (during overdose) coma, heart attack, and death

It's worth spending a moment on the question of amnesia and sedatives. In addition to the relaxation effects of the drugs, many cause at least a minor amount of amnesia. In a medical setting, this can be a benefit; for example, short-term amnesia immediately after surgery can make recovery easier. But in daily life, sedative- or hypnotic-caused amnesia can be a real problem. Users of Ambien, for example, sometimes report not only sleepwalking, but also eating, e-mailing, and even driving while asleep. And in a social setting, sedative-caused amnesia can be terrifying. Predators have been known to slip sedatives ("roofies," or "date rape drugs") to their victims in order to rape or take advantage of them (see sidebar). Victims wake up hours later, uncertain what occurred.

The three most common "date rape drugs" are Rohypnol, GHB, and ketamine.

Some sedatives are extremely addictive, while others are far less so, but they all seem to lead to some degree of tolerance. The CNS is a highly adaptable system—if someone is taking sedatives regularly, his or her CNS will respond by decreasing the amount of GABA it produces naturally. If the person suddenly can't get the drug, he or she will experience withdrawal, which is quite painful, with symptoms including irritability, agitation, and disturbed sleep.

Anti-anxiety and anti-insomnia medications are absolute lifesavers for many people. Current formulations of the drugs are safer than they have ever been. In recent years, however, we've been flooded with TV commercials for various sedatives and hypnotics, all making it sound like these drugs are a risk-free path to total relaxation and blissful sleep. But, interestingly, *Consumer Reports Best Buy Drugs* reported in 2014 that popular prescription sleep aids caused most people to fall asleep only 10 or 20 minutes faster than placebos. It's important to cut through the hype and remember that these are still real drugs with real risks.

TEXT-DEPENDENT QUESTIONS

1. What are some key differences between barbiturates and benzodiazepines?
2. How do sedatives impact the body?
3. Why are sedatives dangerous if used improperly?

RESEARCH PROJECT

Find out about insomnia and the many nondrug methods people can try to help themselves sleep better. Collect information on different strategies (this might include nutritional supplements, improving "sleep hygiene," using melatonin, light therapy, or chronotherapy), and write up a report covering the pros and cons of each method.

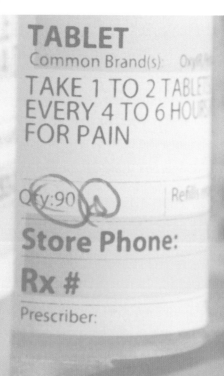

CHAPTER FOUR

STIMULANTS

In this disease of attention . . . every impression seems to agitate the person, and gives him or her an unnatural degree of mental restlessness. People walking up and down the room, a slight noise in the same, the moving of a table, the shutting a door suddenly, a slight excess of heat or of cold, too much light, or too little light, all destroy constant attention in such patients. . . . They say they have the fidgets.

The passage above was written by a doctor named Sir Alexander Crichton in 1798. In a book chapter called "On Attention and its Diseases," he identified a condition of **hyperactivity** and lack of mental focus—or, as he described it, "the incapacity of attending with a necessary degree of constancy to any one object." This condition that was written about over 300 years ago now affects many children, teenagers, and adults. Contemporary doctors call this condition attention-deficit hyperactivity disorder (ADHD).

In 2011 (the most recent year for which solid numbers were available), more than 6 million Americans under age 17 had received a diagnosis of ADHD at some point in their lives. About two-thirds of these individuals

47

were taking regular medication to help manage their condition. In 2012 sales of prescriptions for stimulant medication had soared past the $8 billion dollar mark. The active ingredient in ADHD medication is called a *stimulant*, a medication that helps you feel alert and more focused. For some people, the medication is associated with feeling "revved up." But it can be tempting for people—especially young people—to take stimulants even when they aren't medically necessary.

The U.S. Substance Abuse and Mental Health Services Administration (SAMHSA) estimates that 1.2 million Americans are using prescription stimulants for nonmedical reasons. Students, for instance, sometimes take stimulants to improve their studying (see sidebar, "Study Aids?" on page 56). Stimulants are also used by truck drivers who have to drive long distances without stopping, and by other adults who work long or very late hours.

A BRIEF HISTORY OF ADHD AND ADHD MEDICATION

Although Sir Alexander Creighton was able to identify ADHD symptoms back in 1798, it was a long road to the types of treatments we use today.

Prescription stimulants can make a huge difference in the lives of people with ADHD.

The condition was described more thoroughly by Sir George F. Still, who is remembered as the father of British pediatrics. In a lecture given in 1902, he described certain young patients as having "a defect of moral consciousness which cannot be accounted for by any fault of environment." Still was referring to the impulsivity that is common among kids with ADHD, and his observations about his patients were among the first steps toward understanding this challenging disorder. That said, his suggestion that these symptoms were some kind of moral failing is not a judgment that would be accepted by doctors today.

In the 1920s, it became more common to suggest that attention problems were caused by a physical injury to the brain. What we call ADHD was referred to back then as "minor brain damage" or, a bit later, "minimal brain dysfunction." We now know that ADHD can occasionally be caused by physical injury—but such cases are an extremely small percentage of the overall total.

The *Diagnostic and Statistical Manual of Mental Disorders* (DSM), issued by the American Psychiatric Association, sets the standard for diagnosing problems with the brain. The first edition, published in 1952, did not mention ADHD. A form of ADHD diagnosis did appear in the second edition, in 1968, where it was called "hyperkinetic reaction of childhood." The diagnosis was further refined in the third edition (1980), this time under the name "attention deficit disorder with or without hyperactivity," and again in the fourth (1994), where the now-established term ADHD finally appeared.

The most recent edition, *DSM-5*, was published in 2013 and made some important adjustments to the definition of ADHD. One important change had to do with the age range of people who could be diagnosed with ADHD. Previously, the main focus had been on young children; the *DSM-5* opened up the diagnosis to teens and adults. The *DSM-5* also describes three main presentations of ADHD: (1) predominantly inattentive, (2) predominantly

The *DSM-5* is a diagnostic tool to help doctors determine if a patient has a mental disorder.

hyperactive-impulsive, and (3) combined inattentive and hyperactive-impulsive. Treatment options—and, consequently, prescriptions—will vary depending on which presentation a specific patient has.

TYPES OF PRESCRIPTION STIMULANTS

Just as our understanding of ADHD has evolved over time, so have the treatments. In the mid-20th century, some doctors treated attention problems with a stimulant called benzedrine sulfate. Invented in 1928, benzedrine sulfate was originally created for use as a **decongestant**. A child psychiatrist named Dr. Charles Bradley prescribed it to some of his patients in 1937, and he remarked on their rapid improvement. "The most striking behavior occurred in the school activities of many of these patients," Bradley wrote. "There appeared a definite 'drive' to accomplish as much

MPH (RITALIN) EFFECTS

The Center for Substance Abuse Research at the University of Maryland notes that MPH (Ritalin), like most stimulants, is dose dependent. That means that people will experience varying effects depending on how much is taken. The recommended dose is usually between 5 to 10 milligrams per day, three times a day. Users who become dependent on MPH might take hundreds of milligrams per day, especially as they develop a tolerance.

Effects at low doses:

- appetite suppression
- wakefulness
- heightened alertness
- euphoria
- impairment of voluntary movement
- headache
- irregular or rapid heartbeat
- nausea and vomiting
- skin rash
- drowsiness (in some people)

Effects at high doses:

- exhilaration and excitation
- agitation
- muscle twitching
- dilation of pupils
- confusion
- hallucinations and paranoia
- flushing
- increased blood pressure and pulse rate
- dry mouth
- vomiting
- fever and sweating
- delirium
- seizures, followed by coma
- anxiety and restlessness
- excessive repetition of movements and meaningless tasks
- formication (the sensation of bugs or worms crawling under the skin)

Source: Center for Substance Abuse Research, "Ritalin," http://www.cesar.umd.edu/cesar/drugs/ritalin.asp.

as possible. . . . Clinically in all cases, this was an improvement from the social viewpoint."

Although Bradley had success with his patients, his work was not noticed by other psychiatrists for many years. In part, this was because Bradley was never able to prove exactly why the benzedrine sulfate worked, or exactly which children would benefit from it. Those questions would remain unanswered for several decades.

The next significant drug was methylphenidate, or MPH. Although MPH was first created in 1944, it would not be formally tested on humans for about ten years. Finally, in 1957, MPH was put on the market, sold as a treatment for depression and fatigue. Eventually MPH became famous under its brand name, Ritalin. In low doses, Ritalin is an effective medication for a number of medical problems. It increases wakefulness, suppresses appetite, and can improve mental focus. But it took very little time for it to be misused—there were reports of problems stemming from recreational use at least as early as 1968.

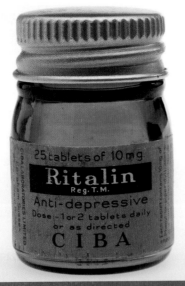

Ritalin was first manufactured by the pharmaceutical company Ciba in 1954.

MPH remains one of the most commonly prescribed ADHD treatments. In addition to Ritalin, MPH is also a key ingredient of several other brand-name medications, including the drugs Focalin, Metadate, Concerta, and the Daytana skin patch.

The single most-prescribed ADHD treatment is not MPH, however, but a specific type of stimulant called an *amphetamine*. This drug is actually a relative of benzedrine,

OTHER ADHD MEDICATIONS

Although stimulants are by far the most common drugs used to treat ADHD, they are not the only ones. Nonstimulant ADHD treatments include:

- atomoxetine (brand name, Strattera)
- clonidine (brand name, Kapvay)
- guanfacine (brand name, Intuniv)

The latter two, clonidine and guanfacine, were originally blood-pressure medications, until doctors discovered they could help some kids with ADHD. Antidepressant medications are sometimes also prescribed.

One key difference between all these drugs and stimulants like Ritalin and Adderall is that these drugs don't cause spikes in dopamine levels in the brain. As a result, they are rarely used recreationally.

from back in the 1930s. It also has chemical similarities to MDMA ("molly"), methamphetamine ("meth"), and even some cold medicines. But this specific blend is prescribed under a brand name you've probably heard: Adderall.

Adderall began life as a 1960s weight loss drug called Obetrol. Obetrol was never very successful, and it was eventually taken off the market. The drug was reintroduced in 1996 under the name Adderall and was marketed specifically for ADHD. Relative to Ritalin and other ADHD medications that were on the market, Adderall took longer to work, but its effects tended to be longer-lasting. This advantage made Adderall a major success. (Other amphetamines that have since been used to treat ADHD have the brand names Dexedrine, Dextrostat, and Vyvanse.)

The arrival of Adderall in 1996 coincided with the publication of *DSM-III*, the first edition to codify the diagnostic criteria for attention-deficit disorder. The late 1990s saw the beginning of a decade-long rise in the number of kids being diagnosed with ADHD and put on some form of medication.

EFFECTS OF STIMULANTS

People using stimulants tend to be more active—they seem more "up" and have lots of energy. This is true whether or not the users have ADHD, which is why the drugs are so ripe for misuse. Prescription stimulants seem to "work" for everyone, whether they are medically needed or not.

That's because stimulants target specific groups of neurotransmitters that all of us have. One is dopamine, the "reward pathway" transmitter that was covered in chapter one. Dopamine is part of a larger group called monoamine neurotransmitters: others in this group include serotonin, epinephrine, and norepinephrine. Epinephrine and norepinephrine are, in a sense, "survival" neurotransmitters—they are part of the "fight-or-flight" response, and they spike whenever a person feels threatened. In ADHD medication, these neurotransmitters help the person feel more focused.

In addition to affecting dopamine and other neurotransmitters, stimulant medication has other effects on the body. The heart rate goes up and blood pressure increases. There is also a spike in glucose, which are sugars that travel in the bloodstream. The **constriction** of blood vessels also means that breathing passages open up. All these physical changes explain why it's so important that ADHD medication only be taken with a prescription. If you take the wrong amount of stimulants—that could mean too much at once, or too often—seizures or heart failure could result. The same is true if you mix ADHD medication with other drugs that have similar effects: for example, cold medication is a very dangerous thing to take with ADHD meds, because the two types of drugs have similar effects.

Over the long term, it's easy to become dependent on the "rush" of stimulants. Tolerance can develop. Once the body comes to depend on the drug, there will be withdrawal symptoms if the drug suddenly isn't available. Symptoms of withdrawal include depression, anxiety, poor sleep, stomach cramps, and exhaustion. Many people report that the withdrawal

People who take ADHD medications need to be careful about what other medications they also take. For example, cold medications frequently have ingredients that are very similar to ADHD medications, which could cause an overdose.

STUDY AIDS?

ADHD medications are used for reasons beyond the "up" feelings they provide. Because they increase mental focus and concentration, many students—especially at the college level—take them in the hopes of improving their grades. But do the drugs work when used this way?

As far as researchers have been able to figure out, the most honest answer is: "sort of, but not really." There is no doubt that stimulants keep people awake. And they do affect the part of the brain that controls concentration—that's exactly why they can be helpful to people with ADHD. People without ADHD find that they can study longer when they take the drugs.

However, no evidence has been found that the drugs make you any smarter, or help you learn more effectively. They just keep you at your desk longer—past the point when your body would probably benefit from a quick nap or a bite to eat! So while people may get a short-term benefit, abusing ADHD drugs probably won't make you a better student. The effects only last a few hours, at which point users have to deal with an unpleasant "coming down" from the drug once it wears off.

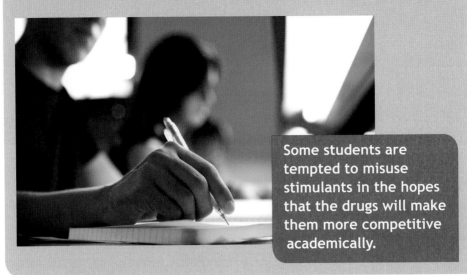

Some students are tempted to misuse stimulants in the hopes that the drugs will make them more competitive academically.

symptoms are noticeably worse than whatever symptoms caused them to take the stimulant in the first place.

Because stimulants affect a person's appetite, long-term use can result in malnutrition. High doses of stimulants, taken over a long period, sometimes cause a mental state that has been described as similar to schizophrenia.

TEXT-DEPENDENT QUESTIONS

1. What are the symptoms of ADHD?
2. Who is likely to misuse stimulants and why?
3. What are the effects of MPH at low doses versus high doses?

RESEARCH PROJECT

Find out more about the ongoing debate over medicating kids with ADHD. Make a list of arguments on both sides: on one hand, what are the risks for kids who might have ADHD but not receive a diagnosis and treatment; on the other hand, what are the risks involved in having too many kids prescribed ADHD medication?

FURTHER READING

BOOKS AND ARTICLES

Anderson, Ann. *Snake Oil, Hustlers, and Hambones: The American Medicine Show*. Jefferson, NC: McFarland, 2000.

Kuhn, Cynthia, Scott Swartzwelder, and Wilkie Wilson. *Buzzed: The Straight Facts about the Most Used and Abused Drugs from Alcohol to Ecstasy*. 4th ed. New York: W. W. Norton, 2014.

Schwarz, Alan. "The Selling of Attention Deficit Disorder." *New York Times*, December 14, 2013. http://www.nytimes.com/2013/12/15/health/the-selling-of-attention-deficit-disorder.html.

Zadrozny, Brandy. "7 Things You Need to Know About Adderall." *Daily Beast*, December 2, 2013. http://www.thedailybeast.com/articles/2013/12/02/7-things-you-need-to-know-about-adderall.html.

ONLINE

National Institute on Drug Abuse. "Prescription Drug Abuse." http://www.drugabuse.gov/publications/research-reports/prescription-drugs.

NDA for Teens. "Drug Facts: Prescription Drugs." http://www.teens.drugabuse.gov/drug-facts/prescription-drugs.

Substance Abuse and Mental Health Services Administration. "National Survey on Drug Use and Health." https://nsduhweb.rti.org/respweb/homepage.cfm.

EDUCATIONAL VIDEOS

Access these videos with your smartphone or use the URLs below to find them online.

 "The Dangers of Prescription Painkillers," ABC News. "Prescription drugs are killing more people than car accidents." https://youtu.be/A001SchjO2U

 "Pill Overkill," SBS One. "Dateline looks at the painkiller abuse that's now reached epidemic levels in the US and could also be heading for Australia." https://youtu.be/wPPRhMudUHU

 "Do These Drugs Make You Smarter?," D News. "Some students are taking 'smart drugs' to perform better in school, but are these drugs actually working?" https://youtu.be/qpZbEC-bLk0

 "Doctors' New Fears Over ADHD Medicine Abuse," CBS This Morning. "There is a new call for immediate action on so-called "lifestyle use" of ADHD drugs." https://youtu.be/9u6PEOjRh_4

 "GenerationRX: Prescription Drug Abuse," Anthony Mennie. "2009 CBI National Student Production Awards Winner: Best Student Documentary." https://youtu.be/IeE8H5WZpGU

SERIES GLOSSARY

abstention: actively choosing to not do something.

acute: something that is intense but lasts a short time.

alienation: a sense of isolation or detachment from a larger group.

alleviate: to lessen or relieve.

binge: doing something to excess.

carcinogenic: something that causes cancer.

chronic: ongoing or recurring.

cognitive: having to do with thought.

compulsion: a desire that is very hard or even impossible to resist.

controlled substance: a drug that is regulated by the government.

coping mechanism: a behavior a person learns or develops in order to manage stress.

craving: a very strong desire for something.

decriminalized: something that is not technically legal but is no longer subject to prosecution.

depressant: a substance that slows particular bodily functions.

detoxify: to remove toxic substances (such as drugs or alcohol) from the body.

ecosystem: a community of living things interacting with their environment.

environment: one's physical, cultural, and social surroundings.

genes: units of inheritance that are passed from parent to child and contain information about specific traits and characteristics.

hallucinate: seeing things that aren't there.

hyperconscious: to be intensely aware of something.

illicit: illegal; forbidden by law or cultural custom.

inhibit: to limit or hold back.

interfamilial: between and among members of a family.

metabolize: the ability of a living organism to chemically change compounds.

neurotransmitter: a chemical substance in the brain.

paraphernalia: the equipment used for producing or ingesting drugs, such as pipes or syringes.

physiological: relating to the way an organism functions.

placebo: a medication that has no physical effect and is used to test whether new drugs actually work.

predisposition: to be more inclined or likely to do something.

prohibition: when something is forbidden by law.

recidivism: a falling back into past behaviors, especially criminal ones.

recreation: something done for fun or enjoyment.

risk factors: behaviors, traits, or influences that make a person vulnerable to something.

sobriety: the state of refraining from alcohol or drugs.

social learning: a way that people learn behaviors by watching other people.

stimulant: a class of drug that speeds up bodily functions.

stressor: any event, thought, experience, or biological or chemical function that causes a person to feel stress.

synthetic: made by people, often to replicate something that occurs in nature.

tolerance: the state of needing more of a particular substance to achieve the same effect.

traffic: to illegally transport people, drugs, or weapons to sell throughout the world.

withdrawal: the physical and psychological effects that occur when a person with a use disorder suddenly stops using substances.

INDEX

ABOUT THE AUTHOR

H.W. Poole is a writer and editor of books for young people, such as the multivolume sets *Mental Illnesses and Disorders* and *Families in the 21st Century* (Mason Crest). She is also responsible for many critically acclaimed reference books, including *Political Handbook of the World* (CQ Press) and the *Encyclopedia of Terrorism* (SAGE). She was coauthor and editor of the *History of the Internet* (ABC-CLIO), which won the 2000 American Library Association RUSA award.

ABOUT THE ADVISOR

Sara Becker, Ph.D. is a clinical researcher and licensed clinical psychologist specializing in the treatment of adolescents with substance use disorders. She is an Assistant Professor (Research) in the Center for Alcohol and Addictions Studies at the Brown School of Public Health and the Evaluation Director of the New England Addiction Technology Transfer Center. Dr. Becker received her Ph.D. in Clinical Psychology from Duke University and completed her clinical residency at Harvard Medical School's McLean Hospital. She joined the Center for Alcohol and Addictions Studies as a postdoctoral fellow and transitioned to the faculty in 2011. Dr. Becker directs a program of research funded by the National Institute on Drug Abuse that explores novel ways to improve the treatment of adolescents with substance use disorders. She has authored over 30 peer-reviewed publications and book chapters and serves on the Editorial Board of the *Journal of Substance Abuse Treatment*.

PHOTO CREDITS

Photos are for illustrative purposes only; individuals depicted are models.
Cover Photo: Dollar Photo Club/JJAVA
Dollar Photo Club: 12 .shock; 19 william87; 21 Burlingham
iStock.com: 7 PeopleImages; 30 Eraxion; 32 bluecinema; 38 cyano66; 40 4X-image; 44 monkeybusinessimages; 55 SelectStock
Library of Congress: 15; 16, 28
Shutterstock: 26 Warren Price Photography; 27 safakcakir; 34 Everett Collection; 48 tomertu; 50 Monkey Business Images; 56 Diego Cervo
UK Ministry of Defence: 29
Wellcome Library, London: 41, 52